2

Marigolds, Myrtle and Moles

Marigolds, Myrtle and Moles

A Gardener's Bedside Book

Written & illustrated by
ALAN TITCHMARSH

H
HODDER &
STOUGHTON

First published in Great Britain in 2020 by Hodder & Stoughton
An Hachette UK company

3

Copyright © Alan Titchmarsh 2020

The right of Alan Titchmarsh to be identified as the
Author of the Work has been asserted by him in accordance
with the Copyright, Designs and Patents Act 1988.

A CIP catalogue record for this title is available from the British Library

Hardback ISBN 978 1 529 31115 0
eBook ISBN 978 1 529 31116 7

Typeset in Celeste by Palimpsest Book Production Ltd, Falkirk, Stirlingshire

Printed and bound in Great Britain by Clays Ltd, Elcograf S.p.A.

Hodder & Stoughton policy is to use papers that are natural, renewable
and recyclable products and made from wood grown in sustainable forests.
The logging and manufacturing processes are expected to conform
to the environmental regulations of the country of origin.

Hodder & Stoughton Ltd
Carmelite House
50 Victoria Embankment
London EC4Y 0DZ

www.hodder.co.uk

For

Debbie Wiseman

with love and thanks

Contents

Introduction

Poetry, perhaps more than any other literary form, is divisive. One man's Seamus Heaney is another's Ogden Nash. What you will find within these pages makes no pretensions to be comparable with the former and pays due homage to the latter.

That's not to say that I am unappreciative of the poet's art; far from it.

I love John Clare's *The Shepherd's Calendar*, and A.E. Housman's *A Shropshire Lad* remains a bucolic favourite. Edward Thomas's verses can make me weep, John Gillespie Magee's *High Flight* really does make my spirits soar, and John Betjeman is invariably a delight. With other poets I must work harder to divine the true essence of their work.

Dystopian views I can do without, for life is a battle to be fought with the sword of determination and the shield of optimism (in perilously short supply of late), rather than the enveloping gloom of relentless defeatism. Angst-ridden poetry has never appealed to me, but then I am of the northern school that believes a problem shared is a problem dragged out till bedtime.

When it comes to amusement and pleasure, the rhymesters offer me instant gratification, whether their work dates back to the seventeenth century, or is current – Stephen Sondheim (a lyricist rather than a poet, though for me the two are synonymous) is the most wondrous wordsmith, as was his Victorian predecessor W.S. Gilbert.

All of the above are considerably greater craftsmen than I am, and I blush even to include their names between the covers of what many will consider to be no more than a collection of rustic rhymes. But they are rhymes with heart, and why should a poem not make you smile, or giggle, or move you to tears, rather than sending you off to ponder on the true meaning of a pattern of words that leave you totally baffled and bewilderingly depressed? There are one or two poems here that do not rhyme, but I hope they have some sort of metre that allows them to qualify.

I also find that I can express my deepest feelings about the fragility of nature and our responsibility to the planet in verse, in the belief that my own delight might perhaps convince others that the natural world really does have something worth discovering and nurturing. Such an approach is sometimes misconstrued.

On more than one occasion I have been described as

being 'relentlessly cheerful', as though it were some kind of failing. Cheerfulness takes effort, especially in this day and age. I would argue that 'determinedly' would be a more accurate choice of vocabulary than 'relentlessly'.

One particular friend of mine is an environmental activist. She tells me that my passion for planting trees and encouraging others to cherish their patch of land, however small, is a waste of time. It comes too late, she says, to make any difference. What is needed is civil disobedience to make the population – and governments – aware of the looming disaster, which will surely engulf us all. It strikes me that my friend is running around sounding a fire alarm; I like to think that I have been steadily manning a hosepipe for the last fifty years.

When I have slunk home, I look upon my orchid-studded wildflower meadow, the wildlife pond I have made, and the garden teeming with birds, bees, butterflies and beetles, and console myself that although my contribution may be small, coupled with that of other like-minded souls I have encouraged over the years, perhaps I have paid some kind of rent for my own existence on earth. My patch at least will help to redress the balance. Surely that is worth something?

These convictions are my excuse for this book.

I have written rhymes for as long as I can remember. I wrote one to accompany a birthday present to my father (a plumber) when I was eleven or twelve. He received it politely but with no comment. I imagine he did not know what to make of either the sentiment or the intention or, come to that, what on earth his son was going to do with his life.

The verses that you will find within these pages are meant to be read out loud; for me, vocal expression helps to mask any literary deficiencies. The odd thoughts that precede them are there to explain their existence, if that seems necessary. They are not meant to be read in one go; rather they are best approached as one would vitamin tablets – at the rate of just one or two a day.

I have a deep and profound love of the natural world – plants and flowers, animals, insects and birds, along with the British landscape – which grows with the years. At the heart of these simple and sometimes cheeky poems you will find, I trust, evidence of that love and an appreciation of the people who have helped to cherish our natural heritage over the years, and a modicum of hope, too. Without it we are doomed to despair, and despair never achieved anything.

My work has often been compared with that of William Wordsworth. Without exception, unfavourably.

Alan Titchmarsh

Why Does the Willow Weep?

'Why does the willow weep, papa?'
Asked the girl with the golden hair.
'Why do its branches brush the ground,
And why are its stems so bare?'

'It weeps for the folly of humankind,'
Said her father with aspect grave.
'Its tears fill the streams and the rivers and seas
At the actions of maiden and knave.'

'And the absence of leaves?' she persisted;
'There are none on its branches today.'
'No; in autumn they yellow and wither and fall,
Then they lie on the ground and decay.'

'Will they ever return?' asked the daughter;
'Has the tree given up now and died?'
Her father looked down at her, then shook his head;
'It is warning us gently,' he sighed.

'A reminder that nothing's forever;
That each living thing has its time.
But with spring you will notice its leaves will return
And under its branches we'll dine

Like we did last summer and the summer before
As the daisies push up from the lawn.
And mama will make biscuits and iced lemonade
As she's done since the day you were born.'

'So all will be well, then, as soon as it's spring?'
Asked the girl with the golden hair;
'For the King and the Queen and the prince and
    princess
And the boy with the pretty grey mare?'

'Yes, all will be well,' said the father;
'There'll be leaves here from May till September;
But the King and the Queen and the boy with the mare
Would do well now to pause and remember

That nature is kindly and weathers the storm,
At least in our lifetime so far;
But one day if we take her for granted too much
She may look on our world and say, "Ah!

These people I shelter and cradle and shade
Give no thought to the oncoming years,"
And her branches once more will sweep down to the
    ground
And the rivers fill up with her tears.

And then in the spring no new leaves will appear
And her wood will turn ashen and brittle;
No birds will be singing, no daisies will flower
Because people cared just too little.'

There were tears in the eyes of the golden-haired girl
At the thought of a world with no trees;
With no singing birds and no daisies below;
No butterflies, beetles or bees.

Her father smiled down at her, ruffled her curls
And said, 'Promise you'll never forget
To take care of all nature as it cares for you;
Only then will your future be set

On a course that is likely to favour the land
And the creatures who on it depend;
Only then will you know, in your mind and your heart,
That we have not hastened the end

Of a world filled with wonder and wild things and love,
Which will make sure this beauty we keep;
And the flowers will bloom and the birds they will sing
And the willow will no longer weep.'

'We will not forget,' said the golden-haired girl
As she gazed on the towering tree;
'We will care for its future; the King and the Queen
And the boy with the mare . . .
Oh . . . and me.'

A COUPLE OF years ago the composer Debbie Wiseman, a friend whom I first met at Classic FM (she is, at the time of writing, Composer in Residence), suggested that she write me 'a signature tune'. Well, it would make a change from that jaunty and supremely catchy theme tune penned by Jim Parker for *Ground Force*.

But there are few opportunities to use a signature tune nowadays, so Debbie came up with the idea of an album with pieces of music composed to represent a number of different flowers – twelve of them, plus a coda (the final cadenza). I submitted a list of trees, plants and flowers about which I felt moved to write verses, and Debbie, with her fertile musical brain, composed a movement for each.

The Glorious Garden, as it was called – a compilation album of my poems and Debbie's music – shot to Number 1 in the Classical Music Charts as soon as it was published, and remained there for several weeks. You'll find all the poems within these pages. I am especially fond of this one:

The Water Lily

Out of reach among reflections
The languid lily lies;
Back against the water,
Gazing at the skies.

Rising up through polished pads
A springboard for the frog;
Pleased to be a lily,
Not a bulrush in a bog.

'Neath its leaves the dragonfly
Will pause to lay its eggs.
Fish can shelter there from sun,
And tadpoles grow their legs.

All this seamy side of life
The lily turns its back on;
Content to see the sun and stars
While other creatures crack on

With the hurly burly things in life
The lily quite ignores;
Cognisant of its beauty
It eschews the daily roars

Of traffic, bees and maybugs,
Preferring just to float
On mirrored pool and lake and pond,
Or clogging up a moat.

Who would bemoan this indolence?
To do so would be silly.
Go vent your spleen on duckweed
And forgive the water lily.

PEOPLE ARE VERY snooty about marigolds – be they French or African or the common Pot marigold that seeds itself about. I suppose it is a combination of their rather stiff habit and the fact that the flowers are either bright orange or yellow – two colours that are out of fashion in 'tasteful' gardens. But marigolds are what gardeners call 'good doers' and I doubt that they give a fig for the feelings of those who prefer their flowers in pastel shades . . .

Marigold

Common? Yeh; some do say that.
Me accent is a pine;
I drops me aitches and me t's,
Can't say, 'The rine in Spine.'

But when it comes to colour,
Ooh! I've got it by the bucket.
And if you can't stand orange flowers,
All I can say is . . . 'Wot a shime.'

OSBORNE HOUSE ON the north coast of the Isle of Wight was Queen Victoria's favourite English home. It was also the house in which she died in 1901. Designed by Prince Albert and Thomas Cubitt, after the fashion of an Italian palazzo, it gazes out across the Solent towards Southampton and Portsmouth.

Planted against one of the towering terrace walls in front of the house is a myrtle, which owes its existence to a cutting taken from a sprig that formed part of Queen Victoria's wedding bouquet. Further sprigs have been taken from it over the years to weave into every bridal bouquet carried at a royal wedding.

To look at the plant, with its unremarkable oval ever-green leaves and fluffy-centred white flowers, you might think it was nothing much to write home about. But you'd be wrong. For the myrtle has history; a history of which it is very proud:

Myrtle

Just because my name is myrtle
Don't imagine that a flirt'll
Conquer me with Cupid's dart;
For history shows I've played my part
In regal matters of the heart.

Back in the days of Queen Victoria,
Along with Vivat and with Gloria,
My place within HM's bouquet,
Carried on her marriage day,
Sealed my place in history.

Since then I have been fiercely loyal
To every bride of family royal;
Carried down the knave and chancel,
Just a peep or sideways glance'll
Show I've grandeur nought can cancel.

Not that I'm in any way
A spectacle to those who may
Remember my important past;
A shrub of a superior caste,
But modest to the very last.

AS A CHOIRBOY back in the 1950s, when I was not reading copies of the *War Picture Library* under cover of the choir stalls, or storing my chewing gum under the hymn-book rest in the introduction to yet another psalm, I would idly make up new words to set to hymn tunes.

The habit continues to this day, with these alternatives to 'Eternal Father, Strong to Save' and 'Abide with Me'.

A Gardener's Hymn

(To the tune: 'Melita' by John B. Dykes)

Eternal Father, cure my doubts
And keep the aphids off my sprouts.
Let weevil, codling moth and flea
Eat someone else's mange-tout pea.
Oh, hear me when I shout and cry
And send a cure for carrot fly.

Make all my courgettes long and fat
And neutralise my neighbour's cat.
Let not my spuds fall prey to blight
Nor rosebuds vanish in the night.
O, hear us when we cry to thee:
For those who garden on TV.

Abide with Me

(The gardener's version; to the tune 'Eventide')

Abide with me, fast fall my spirits, Lord,
My back is aching and I can't afford
Bills from the chiropractor and the doc,
My rotavator's bust, my spade's in hock.

Both of my knees have given up the ghost,
Yet these are not the things that hurt me most.
Decades of wind and rain and searing heat
Seem to have finished off me poor old feet.

Tinnitus reigns from mower noise in my ears,
But this is not the greatest of my fears.
Chilblains on fingers, chapping on my lips,
Soon I'll be needing two replacement hips.

So when at last I walk that garden path;
When I'm in pain, despite the Radox bath;
Lord of the garden, border, flower and tree,
Help of the helpless, oh abide with me.

THOSE SATIRICAL STALWARTS Sir Richard Stilgoe and the
late Peter Skellern were, as a duo, wordsmiths par excel-
lence, and I can listen to and laugh at 'Mrs Beamish' and
'Joyce the Librarian' time after time.

I freely admit that the following was inspired by Joyce
and can be recited to the tune composed by the masters:

Emily the Gardener

Emily the gardener
Had a back yard and a
Window box many admired.
Of her pansies, geraniums,
Fuchsias and lamiums
She never grew weary or tired.

Yet she lived all alone
With no internet, no phone;
In her breast an aching void;
Till Ted the landscaper
(No fags, just a vaper)
Blew smoke into her eyes.

Then Emily's heart
Was quite broken apart
By Ted's bulging dungarees.
Without being tardy
She banished her cardy,
Hoicked her skirt above her knees.

She abandoned her glasses,
Took Pilates classes
Her figure to try and slim down;
For Ted the landscaper
No plans drawn on paper
Was her 'Capability' Brown.

It started quite quickly,
Her stomach felt sickly,
As she worked on her pelvic floor;
Each night as she slept,
Into her mind crept
Such thoughts as were not there
    before.

Up to then in her dreams
She'd seen sweet peas and beans,
Rhododendrons of various sorts;
Now at night in her bed
Swirling round in her head
She saw Ted in his blue boxer shorts.

Ted was doing hard labour
For her next-door neighbour
Transforming a dingy back yard

With a few bits and bobs
Like those make-over jobs
That are so quick they can't be that hard.

He smiled over the railing,
Em leaned on the paling,
And he sashayed across to her side.
He said, 'Yours looks a bit dreary;
Can I help you, me dearie?'
And Em was swept up by a tide

Of abandoned emotion;
She had not a notion
Of what Ted had planned to achieve.
He saw in Em's eyes
Such a glittering prize
And her bosom had started to heave.

As she listened intently,
He wooed her so gently
With words that brought joy and
   delight.
Ted knew he could reach her
Through his water feature
Before day had turned into night.

In the days that ensued,

His quest he pursued

Showing brochures of fountains and rills;

As he pointed out jewels

Of ponds, streams and pools,

Flashing smiles, she went weak at the gills.

There was no 'What the heck'-ing

When he mentioned decking;

Blue fences and cobbles, pergolas;

She would not have sobbed bitterly

At marble from Italy

So smitten was she with Ted's molars.

And so, one week later,

With water to sate her,

Em gazed on a courtyard of class;

The envy of strangers,

Replete with hydrangeas,

A gazebo, a pool made of glass.

But Em's one mistake

With her miniature lake,

The fountain, the statues in pairs,

Was to think that Ted's price

Would reflect she'd been nice
And made biscuits and chocolate
  eclairs.

When his bill came at last
Emily looked on aghast
At the numbers writ large on the page.
How could she have thought
That her cheesecake and torte
Would have somehow discounted
  her age?

Ted's a millionaire now
And has taken a bow
From his decking, and all that palaver;
He now – here's the killer –
Lives retired in a villa
By the sea on the far Costa Brava.

Emily still has the vapours
At the thought of landscapers,
Their patios, paving and cobbles.
Even now, when she gazes
On gazebos and daisies
It brings on the old collywobbles.

She daily avers
The mistake was all hers;
She should never have thought that Ted's smile
Meant that she would rejoice
With a smaller invoice,
She should have seen him coming a mile.

The moral is clear,
From the Tyne to the Wear
From Stoke Poges to Bude and Penberth;
If you engage a builder
From St Mawes to St Kilda,
'Twill like as not cost you the earth.

Spend your money on dahlias
Hostas, azaleas,
Kniphofias, pansies and pinks;
Save those socking big cheques
Spent on patios and decks;
Em will tell you that landscaping stinks.

She's moved now, you know
To a small flat in Bow
For her overdraft won in the end.
She has one hanging basket

With ivy to mask it
But is saving up money to spend

On roses, montbretia,
Nerines, nemesia,
Peonies, tulips and daffs.
'Cos when all's done and said
With a flower in your bed
It's cheaper and you'll get more laughs.

THERE ARE MANY plants we take for granted, in particular those two festive stalwarts *Ilex aquifolium* and *Hedera helix*, more commonly known as:

The Holly and the Ivy

'The holly and the ivy'
At Christmas time we sing;
But they were never bosom friends,
For them the bells don't ring.

The ivy journeys upwards,
Clinging on by questing roots;
The holly bush resents this fact
And doesn't give two hoots

For the ivy's social climbing
Which it thinks is infra-dig;
For holly is a slower grower,
Seldom getting big

Until it reaches middle age
In places it quite likes,
And even then the antisocial
Holly's full of spikes.

You'll never see the two of them
Evincing mutual passion,
For the prickles on the holly
Give the ivy shaving-rash 'n'

Even when it's Christmas and
They're stuffed behind a picture
You can see the holly shrinking
With discomfort at the mixture.

The root cause of the holly's pique
And why its life is pants
Is that male and female flowers
Are both found on separate plants.

Delve deep and at the heart of things
You'll soon detect the reason
That a lack of hanky-panky
Spoils the holly's festive season.

The only time you'll see a holly
Looking gay and bright
Is when it has both flowers
On one plant – hermaphrodite.

With berries red and shiny leaves
It glows in its apparel;
A worthy Yuletide symbol
That we sing of in our carol.

At Christmas, when the mistletoe
You're ducking underneath,
Spare a thought for holly
Stuck with ivy in that wreath.

MAKING A WILDLIFE pond, which I did more than ten years ago now, is an endeavour that has given me more pleasure and satisfaction than any other garden feature. Not only because of its beauty and the reflective qualities of the sheet of water that sits outside my study window, but because of the forms of life it supports, which would otherwise not visit my garden.

Insects in particular – those vital yet underrated and undervalued forms of life – are drawn like a magnet to its surface and its depths. The most spectacular of these are the dragonflies that glide above the water like Lancaster bombers; the sun glinting on their wings, which emit a delicate, fluttering sound, if you get close enough, like that of a stiff breeze upon tissue paper.

The Dragonfly

Sit back and watch the dragonfly:
Is she a Hawker or a Darter?
Pretty soon she'll have to start a
Family and lay her eggs
On sunken stems and so her legs
Will take her backwards down the leaf
Of iris, till she's underneath
The water's surface, safe and wet,
And only then her eggs will get
Conditions that they need to hatch.
And so it's best to have a patch
Of water that is clear and still;
To dragonfly that fits the bill,
For there her young will start their life,
But not as beauteous as the wife
Of her discourteous, handsome male
Whose morals are beyond the pale,
For he is off with roaming eyes
Some other girl to fertilise.
But Mr D's disturbing morals

Don't give rise to family quarrels.
The female has no time for spats;
She's soaring clear of birds – and cats –
In order to preserve the race;
She needs to flit at quite a pace
Depositing her precious ova
Out of sight of thrush and plover.
Marvel at her aerial grace
And find for her a special place
Both in your heart and on your pond.
Of her I am distinctly fond,
She has more style than wasps and drones
Or namesakes found in *Game of Thrones*.
For her I'd write a grand sonata
The Queen of all the Odonata.

IN 1955 THE poet, writer and naturalist Geoffrey Grigson compiled *The Englishman's Flora*, a companion to British wildflowers, which listed the many common names of our native plants – names that vary from county to county. I find it an entrancing book and dip into it regularly to remind myself of the diversity of our botanical riches and the assiduity of Grigson when it came to exhaustive local research.

Did he, perhaps, sit down on a country bench with a hedge layer in Gloucestershire and ask him what he called Cow Parsley in his neck of the woods? The names themselves are a magical litany . . .

Wild Beauty

Campion, goatsbeard, meadow rue;
All of these I offer you,
Along with poppy, meadowsweet
And lady's bedstraw at your feet.

Brush your way through honeysuckle,
Old man's beard and then with luck'll
Come along a clearing paved
With violets, celandine and waved

With plumes of willowherb and sallow,
Clumps of gorse and mounds of mallow.
Drown yourself in Yorkshire fog
And gaze on sundew sprung from bog.

Walk the woodland through the clouds
Of flowering may and beechwood shrouds,
To breathe in tang of spruce and pine
And catch your sleeves on eglantine.

By riverbank and stream and beck
'Neath willow wands and reed mace check
That water blobs, bog bean and lily
All survive – I'm not being silly,

For if we fail to see them bloom
Then surely soon a time will come
When each and every British flower,
Each climbing plant upon its bower

And every orchid, sedge and rush,
Each moss and fern, each tree and bush
Will wither for the want of care,
Since no one noticed they were there;

Or, even worse, were smothered under
Concrete thanks to lack of wonder.
Our world would then be all the poorer
Without our precious British flora.

Gather ye rosebuds, if ye must
But never give your love to just
The cultivated trees and flowers
For nature's blooms are rightly ours

To cherish and to then hand on
To generations when we're gone.
Watch them, love them, serve them well,
Burdock, daisy, pimpernel.

Bluebell, nettle, Queen Anne's lace,
Each one here deserves its place.
Let them thrive and drop their seeds
And never call them 'dreadful weeds';

For weeds are just a man's invention,
Thwarting now his best intention.
Find a spot to show their worth.
Like you, they own a place on earth.

SOME FOLK LOVE topiary – evergreen trees and shrubs clipped into simple or fantastic shapes. Others despise them. I am of the former persuasion, but I do wonder if the plants themselves have feelings – and opinions – about this ultimate form of horticultural control-freakery.

Topiary

Chip, chop,
Snip, snap,
What's a bush to do?
Here he comes with secateurs
Intent on clipping yew.

Orb, cube,
Pyramid,
There's no ifs or buts.
Shear hell it is for questing shoots;
Death by a thousand cuts.

Privet, holly,
Yew and box,
The end result is clear;
All the gardener gives you
Is a clip around the year.

Toytown,
Trumpton;
Never tall and grand.
Oh, the ignominy of it:
Teletubbyland.

FOR THE LAST thirty-odd years I have gardened organically, declining to use any chemical sprays and any inorganic fertilisers. But for as long as I can remember, I have been what is now referred to as a 'wildlife gardener' and, as a result of sharing my plot with other living creatures, my own life and the lives of my family have been enriched beyond measure by the company of birds, butterflies, bees, bats, frogs, toads, newts, dragonflies . . . the list goes on and on.

In addition to the wildlife pond – which we dug – we have a wildflower meadow that I sowed by hand on two acres of ground that we bought from the neighbouring farmer. It delights me afresh every spring and summer, when first the cowslips turn the greensward sulphur yellow.

They are followed by marguerites – or moon daisies if you prefer – then the golden pea-flowered vetches and bird's foot trefoil, yellow rattle, wild carrot and clover push through, to be followed in mid- to late summer by purple greater and lesser knapweeds, frothy white and yellow lady's bedstraw, sky-blue scabious and mounds of soft-purple marjoram in July and August. The colour of this botanical tapestry changes like a natural kaleidoscope.

Ten years on, orchids are beginning to appear – this year we found a bee-orchid and cracked open a bottle of bubbles to celebrate. A pattern of rides is mown through the flowers to allow us to walk among them, and the whole lot is cut down in early September – once the seeds have ripened and fallen – and the 'hay' removed. That is all we do, and the rewards are totally disproportionate to the pleasure.

The joy of all this is tainted only slightly by those forms of wildlife that I would prefer not to play host to. But then, when it comes to wildlife, it is they who choose you, not the other way about. I blame Noah . . .

The Ark

When Noah came to fill the Ark
I wish he'd been aware of stark
Reality when choosing beasts;
Ignoring those I like the least.

Elephants, giraffes and such –
I like them, thank you very much,
But cockroaches, brown rats and
  weevils,
Sundry other insect evils;

Why could he not make a stand
Against Our Lord's almighty hand?
A heaven-sent opportunity
To give us all immunity

From ringworm, leeches, nits and lice.
He can't have thought them all quite nice,
Not least for what they'd do onboard
Infecting all that motley hoard

Of zebras, monkeys, Shem and Ham.
Japheth and his dad and mam
Would wish that he'd have thought
    of that
When stuck up on Mount Ararat.

They could have had a life more
    pleasant,
Thanks to polar bear and pheasant,
Lion, tiger, dog and cat;
But with orang-utan and bat

They harboured tapeworm and
    horseflies –
The sort of things we all despise.
I know that he was under orders
To allow all kinds of boarders;

Not just panda, owl and tortoise
But those things which life has taught us
Make existence jolly tough
For fox and badger, bear and buff-

Alo, who'd rather rub along
With lion's roar and robin's song

Than with blood-sucking parasites
That blight our days and plague our
    nights.

Do you suppose that in that vessel,
Fleas were happy just to nestle
In the fur of stoat and skunk
Asleep in hammock, berth and bunk,

Declining to reveal their aims –
Their sanguinary Olympic Games?
They slumbered deep without a
    murmur
Till landing upon terra firma;

Mandibles and stings and teeth
Were sharpened so they could bequeath
To animals and humankind
The maladies we are resigned

To coping with from hour to hour.
Oh, Noah! It was within your power
To turn away these trials of life,
If you had taxed your lady wife.

If only you had thought to ask
(You know *you* cannot multi-task).
Your missus could have saved the nation
From measles, mumps and constipation.

The tsetse fly, she'd not have borne it;
Vampire bat and Asian hornet,
All would have been shown the door.
She could have been our guarantor

Of health and wealth and life serene,
With skies of blue and fields of green.
But, no, because you couldn't hack it
We have eelworm, leatherjacket,

Chafer grub and codling moth
To make us fume and show our wrath.
And all because, dear Mr Noah,
Your soft heart declined to show a

Preference to creatures pleasant,
So thank you for our birthday present.
Still, I s'pose it must be hard
To take your place in the vanguard

Of those who love *all* forms of life,
Regardless of ensuing strife.
We must defer and beg your pardon
Thank you . . . for our wildlife garden.

The Mole

Nosing up through fibrous loam,
The mole ignores the lure of home.
In spring, when sap begins to rise,
He journeys upwards to the skies

Of blue that mean an end to gloom
For underground there's little room
For candles, lamps and forms of light
That aid the human's power of sight.

Below the crust of rural turf
He bores his way intent on perf-
Orating lawn and putting green
Where groundsmen proud and gardeners keen

Tear out their hair and curse and swear
At piles of earth that were not there
When yesterday they went to bed;
Their velvet sward well-mown, well-fed.

But moley is oblivious
To human ire and human fuss;
He needs clean air within his snout
To force the scent of fungus out.

For though his life is subterranean,
Thanks to his substantial cranium
He can power through the soil
(He's never shirked from honest toil)

Until his tiny eyes are blinking
At the morning sunlight winking
Through the leaves of oak and conker.
Even when he has a stonker

Of a cold in his long nose
Because his home in winter froze,
He battles on; no pause, no rest;
No one to rub Vick on his chest.

And then at last he's broken through
The lawn so loved by me and you.
But stay your trap and leave that fuse
For both would be a cruel ruse

To banish moley from our lives.
'Tis not his fault that he deprives
Us of our joy in groundsmanship
Because, and now I'll let it slip,

There was a time when he preferred
To live in trees just like a bird.
But on high branches he soon found
He felt much safer close to ground.

Up there, among the singing boids,
He felt the need of Polaroids.
So bright the light upon his eye
It made him squint to look at sky

With clouds as white as driven snow;
They'd give poor moley vertigo.
But birds disparaged his position
(There is no avian optician),

So down he came and dug away
Among the holly leaves that lay
Upon the ground on forest floor;
But prickles made his nose so sore

That soon he sought more gentle earth
Through which to burrow, hence the turf
That you and I so carefully mow
Is now his chosen *Mon Repos.*

Waistcoats, trousers, pads for blisters
You will find that some insist as
Fabric they are *sans pareil*;
That makes me sad; it makes me sigh

To think that moley's only use
Is for his fur of greyish hues.
Leave him be to dig and delve
And then congratulate yourselve

S on loving moley for his skill:
A gardener simply born to till
The earth that lies beneath our feet;
That grows our onions, beans and beet.

He needs no spade, he needs no shovel;
Sand and clay that lie above'll
Soon be pushed to make the hills
That bear proud witness to his skills.

He follows on the work of Adam,

Respect him please, dear sir and madam.

Mr Mole deserves a pardon . . .

Unless, of course, he's in *my* garden.

The Wasp

With calamine my skin anoint
And tell me please, what is the point
Of wasps?

They gorge themselves upon my plums;
They sting my children on their bums.
Ow! Wasps.

I watch them chew my garden bench;
My eyes screw up, my buttocks clench
At wasps.

They cause my visitors alarm
As they repel with flailing arm
The wasps.

You ask, 'Oh death, where is the sting?'
It's in the rear end of that thing:
That wasp.

Summer picnics are a farce
Because of that thing in their . . . bottom;
Damn wasps!

I try to swat 'em, try to clout 'em,
Life would be so nice without 'em;
Wasps.

Remember every little creature
Is a worthy garden feature;
. . . Every little creature that is except that yellow stripy
insect, which has the capacity to completely ruin an
otherwise perfectly blissful summer afternoon in my
garden by buzzing round the heads of my guests and
driving them to distraction until we are forced to go
indoors to get away from them.

Huh! Wasps.

The Slug

'Repugnant' is the word that's used
To blame a creature so abused
By gardeners throughout the land;
With snails they form a slimy band

Of molluscs, who lush plants devour.
They use their rasping tongues to scour
At leaves of seedling plants and hostas
And in so doing they will cost us

Evenness of mind and temper;
Mollusc motto: *Munchit semper.*
It's clear to me that they are able
To decipher every label

On a plant that shows its price;
Expensive ones are twice as nice.
They never take the cheap and cheerful
Leaving gardeners sad and tearful.

As if to magnify their lark
They only visit after dark
Imagining that this ruse spectacular
Brackets them with one Count Dracula.

I'd rather have an ugly bug
Than any slimy, slothful slug.
They may move slowly on their slime
But plants will vanish in no time

Thanks to their mammoth appetite.
Delphiniums are their Vegemite.
In gardens poor or gardens posh
Just use your welly-boot to squash

This enemy of bed and border;
Nasty, slithery marauder.
Oh dear, I seem quite overwrought;
Forgive my violent train of thought,

It's just that when it comes to slugs
I look on them as garden thugs.
Although I know I'll never beat 'em;
It's such a shame that we can't eat 'em –

Gently fried in olive oil
Or put in brine and left to boil.
They really are beyond the pale
But then . . . well, there's the bloody snail!

THANKS TO *Downton Abbey*, most folk are now aware of the existence of the majestic Cedar of Lebanon, even if they do not realise it, for these are the trees under which the Earl of Grantham walks with his Labrador in the opening credits of the television series. The Earl's cedars are, in reality, at the *real* Downton – Highclere Castle – home of the Earl and Countess of Carnarvon.

They have always held a particular magic for me, being possessed of elegance, grace and presence, as well as surviving for centuries.

Cedar of Lebanon

Grandee of the stately park,
Yet stranger to the town,
Owned by Marquess, Earl and Duke;
Advised by Mr Brown.

'Neath velvet arms spread high and wide
In shades of sober green,
Twelve generations watched you grow;
Three hundred years you've seen.

Eight monarchs crowned within your reign
On Britain's rolling dales,
And still you stand steadfast in England,
Ireland, Scotland, Wales.

A noble, silent watchful life
While all around decay;
Calm through pestilence and war,
Triumphant still today.

O cedar, with your sturdy frame
Let those who gaze in awe,
Remember with respect and pride
All those who went before.

The men with spades who never knew
Your majesty mature;
Let us give thanks and celebrate
The gardeners of yore.

ANTICIPATION IS PART of the joy of gardening: waiting for the first asparagus in April, longing for the cherry blossom to open and drown us in 'snow'.

In the lean-to barn that shelters a gypsy caravan we have had since the girls were young, and where we made sausage sandwiches on the little stove after the fashion of Roald Dahl's *Danny: Champion of the World*, there is that moment when the swallows return from overwintering in Africa and decide whether or not to make their summer home with us in the rafters above the vardo . . .

Swallows

Will they, won't they?
They're looking . . .
Wheeling over the barn shrieking, 'We're back,
    we're back!'

They're in . . . they're out . . .
Wittering.
'Shall we? Shan't we?' There are other places to
    see as well . . .

They scout, we hope . . .
Please stay . . .
They did last year, but will they choose to
    return?

Two hundred miles a day . . .
It's a lot.
From South Africa to Hampshire – over a month
    and a half of flying.

Twitter, witter . . .
Yes or no?
They circle, they dip inside, they come out, they go

They go . . . and they go.
They don't return.
Not this year, then; this year others will enjoy their
    company.

When swallows stay
We have frivolity.
Without them the barn above the caravan is quiet,
    hollow.

Perhaps next year.
We wait and hope.
Please come back. The barn is ready. We miss you.

I LIKE TO think that I am not, by nature, chippy, but every so often that human trait gets the better of me and – until I can reason with myself and banish the unworthy feelings of grumpiness – I will have a few moments of festering about something that niggles. 'Move on, move on,' my conscience tells me. Wisely.

To be embittered is to find oneself eaten away from the inside until nothing but a hollow carapace remains. I don't want that. I've seen enough examples of it to realise the futility of such introspection.

That said, there is one little recurring niggle that keeps raising its ugly head. I fight it, but it will keep popping up . . .

A Place in History

I muse from time to time on why I'm here;
On whether there's a plan within this sphere
That I am some small part of, so to speak.
And then I ask myself . . . am I a freak?

The ego bit is worrying, I confess;
My upbringing taught me to believe I'm less
Than qualified to claim I play a part
In encouraging all folk to make a start

On that piece of ground o'er which they hold their
   sway.
I try most ev'ry week, nay, ev'ry day
To get across to anyone who'll listen
That gardening still gives me quite a frisson.

I joined a band of populists, I know;
Whose work will doubtless melt like summer snow,
But should I worry that in history,
My name will count for nothing more than mystery?

I read, you see, of gardening in Britain
In books that have been eminently written
By gardeners who are . . . now, how can I put it?
Well, gardeners considered 'classy', but it

Can't just be for the upper-middle classes;
These gurus who have absolutely masses
Of land they shape, design and somehow order,
But who will seldom ever see a *tiny* border.

They're revered, quite rightly, in the glossy pages
Of books and magazines throughout the ages;
Their names will figure much on Hatchards'
    shelving,
But when it comes to digging and to delving

In gardens found in street and cul-de-sac,
Or with veggies on allotments out the back,
The baskets and the boxes and the pots:
The 'gardens' of the folk who don't have lots

Of space that they can call a grand estate,
Why don't they get a mention? What's their fate?
The history of gardening in our isles
Should acknowledge those who don't own country piles.

I'm not a rampant leftie – heavens above!
But millions of gardeners who love
To grow their own and cherish tiny patches
Deserve at least a mention in dispatches.

The folk who now pass on this earthly passion
Will doubtless be quite overlooked by fashion.
But when that one great scorer looks on land,
I hope he won't just lavish praise on grand

Designs that are the product of the gentry;
But value, too, the very modest entry
Into gardening that's found round humble dwelling;
They have no Aga, just a Baby Belling.

So when next you thumb the pages of a glossy
Book that seems inordinately bossy
And shows gardens that *you'd* call a National Park,
Designed for Celeb, Earl or Oligarch,

Just remember that that little plot in Bristol,
Or Cleethorpes or West Brom or South Uist'll
Matter every bit as much in Stoke or Leeds
To gardeners who take cuttings and sow seeds,

As a plot of several acres in the Shires,
Or in Belgravia, with pleached hornbeams trained on
    wires;
What matters – tell your friends and all your rellies,
Is not the brand or colour of your wellies

But the callouses upon your horny hand,
Which show that you're a lover of the land.
That you can grow a cabbage or a dahlia,
And relish your success and admit failure.

Don't imagine that you've gone and missed the boat
If all you have's a pot in Swadlincote.
The allotment down in Penge or Tooting Bec
Is as valuable as gardens of high spec

That are talked about among the chattering classes.
To you it is we gardeners raise our glasses.
Keep growing things and know their proper worth.
You are – I reckon – pure salt of the earth.

THE BINOMIAL SYSTEM of botanical nomenclature devised by Carl von Linné (better known as Linnaeus) is the bane of many would-be gardeners' lives. 'I'll never be a gardener!' they wail. 'I just can't remember those Latin names.'

Such difficulty should not put anyone off, although those of us who garden for a living use them as our own *lingua franca*. As the years go by, it is somewhat embarrassing for older gardeners to discover that the Latin names of plants are easier to retain than the English names of people.

Latin names are useful, in that they are universal, though what nobody tells you is that their pronunciation from country to country and continent to continent varies considerably. You will need a particularly keen ear if holidaying in Bavaria, for instance, to work out that Sass-ee-fragga ite-so-ee-dez is, in fact *Saxifraga aizoides*.

The Germans also have a rather embarrassing way of pronouncing the Latin name of the pine tree – Pinus. We say it to rhyme with 'minus'. They say it to rhyme with 'Venus' – especially embarrassing if they are vocal when admiring your fine specimen.

As a student gardener, struggling to remember such

names for a living, we had silly ways of committing them to memory, such as setting them to music. One confection that particularly sticks in my mind is set to the tune of *La Donna et Mobile*, from Verdi's *Rigoletto*:

Parthenocissus tricuspidata
Thuja plicata;
Pinus sylvestris
Hamamelis mollis;
Magnolia grandiflora
Tilia euchlora
Metasequoia glyptostroboides,
Rhus typhina.

Gomphrena globosa
Nepeta nervosa
Lavatera trimestris
Geranium sylvestris
Liatris spicata
Thujopsis dolabrata
Clematis viticella 'Purpurea Plena Elegans'
Viscum album.

Ah, Verdi, how you would have loved that – especially as it ended with mistletoe . . .

JAPANESE MAPLES SELL on sight in spring, when in garden centres across the land, they unfurl their delicately fingered leaves. They are taken home and planted in fits of optimism. Sometimes this is justified and they thrive; on other occasions they show their displeasure. It's all down to growing conditions really.

Japanese Maple

Elegant,
Inscrutable,
Tricky,
Prone to scorch.

Best by water gardens;
Unsuitable for porch.

Finely cut,
Filigree,
Palmate,
Slow of growth.

Hates the wind and hates the sun;
A martyr to them both.

Bonsai,
Ikebana,
Origami
(No; that's paper)

On sandy soil a nightmare,
On solid chalk a caper.

Indispensable,
Essential,
Divine,
A must-have cutie.

The geisha of the garden,
An oriental beauty.

I HAVE A great fondness for sweet peas, not simply because they are obliging annuals with wonderfully fragrant flowers, but because of a faded photograph I have of my grandfather leading me by the hand – aged one-and-a-half – through rows of them growing up bean poles on his allotment by the River Wharfe in Ilkley.

I like to think I can remember the occasion vividly, though I am probably being lulled into that sense by the photo itself. Nowadays I grow them on my own vegetable patch for cutting, and I marvel at their ability to oblige every bit as much as I did when I was knee-high to my grandfather.

Sweet Pea

The sweet pea is a scented climber
And, as such, it's hard to rhyme a
Nother word with fragrant, innit?
Give me just another minute . . .

To find 'flagrant' (not the word;
This legume's not the common herd).
It climbs by tendrils into space
Possesses delicacy, grace.

Cut the flowers oft and never
Let it seed or you will ever
Rue your folly – flowering stops;
You might as well grow wheat or hops

If you cannot appreciate
The fragrance of this opiate
Whose heady scent will fill the air,
Whose flowers cause all folk to stare

At frilly blooms of pink and blue,
Of white and yellow, carmine, too.
But dip your nose towards their petals
And you'll be stung as sharp as nettles

By a perfume sweet but light,
Strong by day but weak by night.
Beloved of the pollen beetle,
Only then you'll find your feet'll

Shuffle off to other flowers
Where no unpleasant insect cowers.
Poor sweet pea to suffer thus
And make the flower arranger cuss.

Still, in summer, who'd concede
A flower that grows each year from seed.
Sow 'em, grow 'em, pick 'em please.
There's nowt on earth to beat sweet peas.

SOME FOLK SIMPLY refuse to grow peonies because of their short flowering season. But they are so spectacular in bloom, with those massive, blowsy flowers, that I find them irresistible – especially when they are grown in rows in a kitchen garden for cutting.

They can be temperamental – refusing to flower if their fat, yam-like roots are buried more than half an inch below the surface of the soil, but once happy they will be content to stay in the same place for years, and positively resent disturbance.

They are stately flowers, and in the class system of garden plants, they rank as the aristocracy.

The Peony

Behold the powdered dowager,
Her hair rinsed candy pink;
Bouffant, lacquered, curled and teased,
Her bosom swathed in mink.

Ample of proportions,
She teeters on her heels,
Her feet are large, her legs are thin,
She's far too fond of meals

Of caviar, asparagus,
Smoked salmon, artichoke;
She'll wash them down with Chardonnay
And sometimes Diet Coke.

She revels in the season,
By the end of June she's gone;
She'll manage Royal Ascot
But seldom Wimbledon.

To some her brief appearance
Means she's vilified and spurned
But others think her grandeur compensates,
Her place is earned

Among the gentry of the border
Where campanulas are girls;
They may have bells and whistles
But the peony has pearls.

Three years after planting
Those campanulas need lifting;
The peony on the other hand
Has roots that take some shifting.

She'll fight against removal
To some other patch of loam,
The spot in which she's planted
Will become her stately home.

For generations there she'll sit
Rejoicing in her bulk;
Suggest to her she could downsize
And all she'll do is sulk.

Not for her the Dower House
To make room for her heir;
Her roots go back centuries,
She's staying put.
So there!

Verse and Worse

Sometimes

    on Waterloo station

        I go

           to the bookstall

            and look

              for poetry books

  I found one

      yesterday

    It had poems

        in it

Well

    it said

      they were poems

All I could

    see

      were words

        . . . not particularly special words . . .

      spaced out

    like this

on very nice paper

        with no punctuation

Funny what some people call poetry.

I AM ASSIDUOUS about pulling up ragwort from my wild-flower meadow, in spite of the fact that I have no livestock. I reason that one day I might, or that a future owner will keep horses in my meadow and ragwort will then be undesirable.

But, in the great scheme of things, every plant has its reason for being, and its own particular wildlife to support . . .

Ragwort

'No one likes me.
No one cares,'
Said ragwort to two passing hares.

'Here I stand,
My head erect;
A testament to man's neglect.

Horses eat me,
Riders quake;
I give their mounts bad stomach ache.

They tell me that
Abandoned acres
Send some horses to their makers.

What can I do?
What can I say?
It's just that I was born this way.

Horsey folk may
Moan and scoff;
My alkaloids quite p**s them
  off,

But just remember
As I die
That some things do on me rely.

You've seen 'em
On those sunny days,
Crawling o'er my golden rays.

Their wings are black
With spots of red;
Thanks to me their eggs are fed,

At least three hundred
At a go
Are laid beneath my leaves and so

If I'm to die,
That insect goth,
The black and crimson cinnabar moth

Would die as well,
Its food departed.
Are you feeling still cold-hearted?'

THANKS TO THE invention of the internet, I now receive very few letters from readers and viewers. Instead they endeavour to reach me by email – a form of communication that, while 'being there forever', is likely to disappear among a welter of spam and far less likely to give lasting joy. I have kept a handful of the more choice missives that have arrived over the years and which still make me smile.

I write letters myself – with a fountain pen and on proper writing paper. It saddens me that in the future we are unlikely to have books compiled from correspondence, for they make wonderful bedtime reading – William Shawcross's *Counting One's Blessings: The Selected Letters of Queen Elizabeth the Queen Mother*, or Deborah Devonshire and Patrick Leigh Fermor's *In Tearing Haste* are a delight, and going back further, the countless volumes of letters written by Horace Walpole – and offer a strong flavour of the life and times of the writers.

Such books are also put-downable when one's eyes begin to close, rather more readily than a book comprised of long chapters during which I invariably nod off before finishing.

Nowadays the producers of television programmes set much store by the reaction of viewers on Twitter. They will sit in the studio gallery and pore over their mobile phones while a programme is being transmitted, instantly relaying the comments of viewers to the colleagues around them as though they were the gospel truth.

I find it ironic that in my early days of broadcasting, viewers' letters – coming from someone who had gone to the trouble of finding a pen, a piece of writing paper, an envelope, a stamp and the address of the person to whom they wished to write – were treated with disdain. (And they were not always written in green ink.) Such correspondents had made a much greater effort – and were probably far more measured in their comments – than the trolls who manage to make their presence felt so readily by tweeting their knee-jerk reactions.

That said, not all the letters I received were on paper designed to be written on, or couched in such terms as led me to believe that my correspondents were especially literate. What they did have in common was that they were all written by someone who was moved enough to take the trouble to send me a letter. Though sometimes I did wonder why . . .

The extracts from the letters shown below were all sent to me via a newspaper, my publisher, a television or a radio programme. They are all genuine and they were all replied to, though whether my replies satisfied those who sent them I seldom discovered. I have removed the names of the senders to avoid embarrassment . . .

Letters

Dear Mr Titchmarsh,

I thought you might like to see how far-reaching your influence is becoming. My niece Emma will be 4 in January. She has recently begun attending pre-school every afternoon, where she has been starting to learn about God. The first afternoon the subject was introduced, she didn't seem too sure about the whole concept. She listened as the teacher explained how God had created the world, but when the teacher said that God created the plants and the trees, she said:

'No – that's Alan Titchmarsh.'

*

Dear Mr Titchmarsh,

I am writing to ask if you have any ideas how I could put bubble wrap into my 6ft by 6ft greenhouse. I usually put green plugs in, but it's such a boring, horrible way. Could there be a much simpler way – i.e.

by making panels and slotting them into place maybe?
What could I use as frames?

I watch your programmes. Please don't ask me to
come on TV as I am not feeling too well.

*

Dear Sir,
Two questions:

What was the mixture you were adding Cointreau
to?

And please may we have the recipe for your
pancakes.

(I did not reply to that one.)

*

An early letter from a nine-year-old viewer:

Dear Nationwide,
Why does Alan Titchmarsh always have clean hands
and boots?

*

Dear Alan Titchmarsh,

Daddy has made the garden an awful mess. Please can you make are garden into a courtyard?

Thank you.

From

Jack

Please come to this address . . .

P.S. I've got a dead rabbit in my garden. It's buried by the big conifer tree. Please don't dig him up. Thank you.

*

Dear Alan,

Watching a recent programme, you mentioned your three pet hates – kinking hosepipes and wire coathangers that tangle. The third one was toilet rolls with inadequate perforations.

I bet you, Alan, that your wife was tempted to buy the quilted ones, which are hopeless. Not only do they shred off when trying to tear off one's requirements, but disintegrate upon the slightest contact with moisture.

Apart from that, me being a very old OAP, I watch my pennies and they are definitely very poor value. I've measured everything!

*

Dear Mr Titchmarsh,

I wonder if you would be interested in helping me?

I am trying to sell my house. It is a nice house but the estate agent says that people do not like the garden. I do keep the garden looking nice, but it is the shape and size that is putting people off.

Can you please come round and see what you could advise?

*

Dear Alan Tit Marsh,

Thank you very much for giving up your time to come to our school to plant some trees. I found it very interesting and complicated. I was amased at how long it took to make such a short piece of film it was very exciting but a bit boring at times.

*

Dear Alan,

I am writing to ask if it was you who I was in a lift with at Presto's in Bognor today.

*

Dear Alan,

This is just a brief note to say please grow your hair again. It suits you so much better long. Your present style makes you look rather like a cheeky schoolboy and if you want to maintain your sex symbol image please bring back the floppy fringe!

*

Dear Alan,

I am a 45-year-old tenor employed by British Gas . . .

*

Dear Alan,

I have a lovely friend, Mary, who has plastic intestines and saw *El Cid* 30 times . . .

*

Dear Mr Titchmarsh,

I am not in the habit of writing fan letters, in fact I have not done so since 1982. I am 37 and have a small front garden and large enclosed back garden. I march about on crutches or a stick, or walk unaided in my support boots when not too pissed. I tumble easily but have yet to fall into my pond est. 1 year, of which I am very proud. I live on a 'problem' council estate and have a prostitute in the upstairs of my duplex. Apart from that I am fine.

I am a huge admirer of Miss Dimmock also.

I like Madonna too.

I own 'The Essex Puma' whom I collected from the Cats' Protection League. After 4 years or so he has tamed me.

I have two rabbits (free range): Susan – who can swim, and Flopsey, who is neutered. He has had much tragedy in his short bunny life – 2 wives and several babies lost to the fox and one to a firework display (heart attack one assumes).

My tortoise Twinkletoes (ageless) is well happy.

Still, enough about me.

How about a signed copy of your novel?

I can send a cheque or VISA.

Alternatively you can have my first fabric painting

on a designer jacket. It's a portrait of you, but you'd
have to iron it.

All the best . . .

*

Dear Mr Titchmark,

I hope I am spelling your name correctly. That's how it
sounds to me on the radio but I have a hearing
problem. A few weeks ago I wrote suggesting an Idea
to the producer of your programme but I did not get a
reply so I repeat the Idea which is a method of
controlling slugs in the garden without the use of
poison. It is only suitable for flat land.

The Idea is to surround the garden with a
permanent miniature moat say 6in deep made from
whatever is suitable and available in your area. If the
moat was, say, 1ft wide and you could control all the
slugs in your garden, the moat would prevent
reinfestation. The moat could be kept topped up by
rainwater from roofs and bathwater. If a storage tank
could be rigged up on the house roof then the gardener
could irrigate from his moat using 1 or 2in diameter
siphon pipes.

Yours sincerely . . .

P.S. Unfortunately, for various reasons, I am at present unable to put my idea into practice.

*

Alan,
Could you please tell me the proper pronunciation of the word 'PLANT'. You always say it as it is spelt. Why is it that the toffs pronunciate it as 'PLARNT' like 'AUNT'?

*

This next epistle was written on the back of the buff envelope in which the query arrived:

IF THIS IS NOT THE CORRECT ADDRESS FOR THE TV SEX-GOD THAT IS ALAN TITCHMARSH PLEASE RETURN THE ENCLOSED IN THE STAMPED ADDRESSED ENVELOPE PROVIDED WITHIN.
  THANK YOU.

*

And finally, a letter accompanied by a small, rigid plastic wallet, which appeared to be filled with gravy:

Dear Alan,
Can you please identify these berries, which were found in the crops of several pigeons shot this week.

GAZE UPON AN English oak growing in a field or in park-land, and you gaze upon a majestic and long-lasting tree, but also one that has shaped our country and led us to where we are today. Yes, well . . . things would have been far worse without it.

English Oak

Rule Britannia, we all sing,
A tribute to the Queen or King
Who rules our shores
And wears our crown.

Though if 'twere just, and truth to tell,
That honour should be shared as well
By yonder tree that grows so strong
In field and hedgerow just along
From sheep and cows that safely
   graze
The meadow in the summer's haze.

The English oak: our saviour who
Built ships that we might take a crew
Of sailors out into the main
To save our shores from those who'd gain
A foothold on our sceptered isle;
Who'd hold their sway by strength and guile.

Who, in their ships so fully manned,
Would force their will upon our land
If not repelled by salty folk
In vessels made of English oak.
Led by Nelson and by Drake
They ploughed the waves for England's sake.

But underneath the cannon's roar
The oaken hull did rather more
Than keep afloat the sailors who,
For Blighty, many a foeman slew.
The ships they sailed and loyally manned
Had roots that sank into their land.

Against the oaken wood and knot
Rattled cannon ball and shot.
Sturdy schooner, brig and galleon
Resisted many a rapscallion;
Till, listing home at battle's end,
They took their rest too lame to mend.

Their timbers now would be relieved
Of warring duties and retrieved
By joiners, carpenters and men
Who built the houses of the gentry;

Beams and joists of English oak,
Their duty done, would now give folk
A roof to keep them dry at night;
A respite from the watery fight.

Think on when next you walk a plank
Upon the floor in house of rank;
For once it may have sailed the seas
With Rodney, Anson, Bligh and these
Are men who knew they should salute
The tree more powerful than Canute.

From acorn small within your hand
Will grow the strongest in the land.
A tree in which we put our trust
When fighting battles fair and just.
It built the houses of our nation,
Made our fame and reputation.

Standing now in hedge and field;
Reminder that we would not yield.
Steel and iron in furnace heat
Cannot with its strength compete;
Cruisers powered by oil and coke
Have not the spirit of the oak.

Plant it for Britannia's sake
So generations hence can make
Their houses, too, from close-grained wood,
And casks to hold a wine that's good;
So they can raise a glass and say,
'Thank God for English oak!
Hooray!'

SOME PLANTS ARE so delicate it's a wonder they survive at all, especially if they are condemned to grow in challenging circumstances. Who in their right mind would expect a delicate beauty like the snowdrop to battle through snow and ice to display its flowers in frosty winter air?

Ah, but the snowdrop is equipped with leaf tips of prodigious strength that can prise their way through frozen earth. They remain, bless them, a wonder of nature. But they probably don't enjoy life much.

Snowdrop

'It's dark down here
And rather cold,'
Said the bulb
Beneath earth's mould.

'I'm only little.
I can't hope
To push up there;
I just can't cope.

If it were summer,
Nice and warm,
I'd gladly leave
My wintry dorm.

But now I'm perished,
Frozen stiff;
My blood's run cold;
In just a jiff

I'll prob'ly die
And that's the truth;
Cut off in me prime,
Me youth.'

'Oh, get a grip!'
A voice rang out.
It was a sturdy
Brussels sprout.

'I'm up here,
Me roots in mud,
Frozen to
The very bud.'

'But you're a vegetable.'
'Yes; that's true.
But just as cold
And fed as you.

So stop your whingeing,
Brace your root
And shove aloft
Your sturdy shoot.'

The snowdrop pushed
(He knew he must)
His leaves and flower
Through frozen crust.

A ray of sunshine
Caught his bloom;
Cheered him
In the wintry gloom.

Just then he heard
Across the garden,
A sound that made
His arteries harden.

Snap, snap; plop, plop;
Children's shouts.
The harvesting
Of Brussels sprouts.

Glancing o'er
Towards the rustle,
The snowdrop saw
The naked Brussel.

Tall and thin
In sea of mud,
The sprout forlorn
Had not a bud.

The snowdrop listened,
Heard it weep;
A client for
The compost heap.

So when you see
The snowdrop flower,
Gaze upon it;
Praise its power

To hold its blooms
In wintry sun;
Then bend right down
And say, 'Well done!'

As for the sprout
On Christmas Day,
Boiled and eaten,
Thrown away.

Living life
Upon the edge;
The fate of any
Common veg.

Cook it, eat it,
Sit down, flop.
And smile upon
The brave snowdrop.

IT IS NOT only the snowdrop that is brave enough to open its flowers when most garden plants – and gardeners come to that – are slumbering deep. The witch hazel – a native of North America, China and Japan, depending on the species – has the most fragile spidery-looking flowers that would seem to be far too delicate to cope with snow and ice.

But cope they do, and cheer us up when there is little else to admire in the winter garden.

Witch Hazel

'When self-respecting spiders,
Proper arachnids, my dears,
Are fast asleep and dreaming,
Then the witch hazel appears.'

This story, it was told me
By an aged maiden aunt;
I've no reason to doubt it
(I've tried to, but I can't).

She said:
'In winter, on bare branches,
Hamamelis flowers pose;
Regardless of the freezing cold
They tantalise the nose

With a scent of summer citrus
That can come as quite a shock;
They sit like wiry spiders
That no icy blast can knock.

Upon the shuttlecock of stems
These fragile-petalled floozies
Disport themselves in tones of gold
(They're also good for bruises).'

Well, not the flowers, but the sap
If we are being picky;
Bought in bottles sold at Boots
(Aunts do not take the Mickey.)

So if you've knocked your head or
   knee
Just open up the bottle;
A little dab for smaller bumps,
For larger ones a lot'll

Make a difference to the pain you feel
On joint and head and limb;
But if your heart is aching
Then those flimsy flowers are simply

Waiting to uplift you,
Just as Auntie said they would.
Aunties and witch hazel:
Two forces . . . for good.

HAVING COMPOSED TWELVE different pieces of music for *The Glorious Garden,* Debbie Wiseman asked for a tailpiece – a coda – and this is it:

The Glorious Garden

From Mother Earth, the silent force
Of all that grows; the only source
Of sustenance for man and beast
Comes food and drink and floral feast.

Disparage not their brilliant hues,
But give them each their rightful dues;
For they alone enrich the land,
The soul, the spirit and the grand

Designs of those who'd shape the earth
To please man's senses. Know their worth
And value, too, the gardeners' craft;
They sowed the seeds while others laughed

At simple work – no brain required –
Just artless labour until tired.
But if they knew what love, what care
Is lavished upon landscape bare,

From far Caithness to deepest Devon,

Creating here a glimpse of heaven,

They'd doff their caps and beg our pardon,

Joyful in the glorious garden.

THOSE OF US who are committed to gardening as a voca-
tion, career, occupation – call it what you will – are hugely
encouraging of others to join us in, quite literally, the best
job on earth.

Gardening is all about learning how plants grow, their
likes and dislikes, the breadth of material available to us
and how it can best be used for our benefit and that of
the planet as a whole. Such knowledge takes a long time
to accumulate – usually involving years of hands-on expe-
rience – but there are those who decide, right from the
start, that they want to be garden designers, rather than
just gardeners.

Some of them . . . how can I put this delicately? . . .
are ladies of a certain age and a certain social class. A few
of them turn out to be quite good at it, but many of them,
I'm afraid, find they have bitten off rather more than they
can chew.

This is the story of one of them:

The Garden Design Course

Week 1

Rupert said I really should do something with the
hours
That I have now both the young have flown; he knows
. that I like flowers.

So I toddled off to Chelsea and a house in Cheyne
Walk,
Where they teach we lady gardeners how to draw and
plan and talk

To other ladies like ourselves who just don't have a
clue
About hellebores and irises and who only need a
few

Ideas on what's appropriate for planting round the
house
And the sort of shapes one uses to impress one's
friends . . . and spouse.

Week 5

Rupert says that my designs must rank among the
  best;
He tells me soon I'll be as good as Vita
  Sackville-West.

I've told him he should come with me and meet our
  tutor, Guy,
But Rupert's meetings mean he gets home much later
  than I.

Week 10

Rupert's in the city; he likes living on the edge,
But at least it means the hedge fund can be used to
  fund the hedge.

Heigh-ho, I mustn't grumble – if I did, I'd be a fool,
And with Flavia and Orlando now away at boarding
  school,

It's good that I have something here – the garden is my
  haven
And we had a talk last week from that delightful Sarah
  Raven.

I adore her taste in colours and, while walking with the
dog,

I find myself just itching to get at her catalogue.

Week 15

Guy says it's quite important that we learn the Latin
names,

So that clients take us seriously and don't think we're
playing games.

My weekends now, when Rupert's here, are just so
swiftly gone.

He said today, quite harshly, 'Who the hell is Monty
Don?'

I hope he's not regretting that I'll have my own
career:

Designing gardens for my friends – the ones who live
quite near.

Week 20

My drawing is improving and my colour schemes are
fine.

The Latin names that I can spell now number twenty-
nine.

I avoid those ghastly yellows – oh, and orange, red . . .
   and puce.
Instead pale blues and pinks and whites are what I
   always choose.

Then OKA's garden furniture – I simply love it all.
Paint colour? Guy says don't be rash, best stick with
   Farrow and Ball.

Week 25
I had my first commission just last week from my
   friend Lottie;
She said her patio and pond were looking rather grotty.

I had to tell her gently that like DDT and Derris,
No one has a patio now, we all call it a terrace.

She looked a trifle cross at that (her temper is volcanic),
So I thought I'd make no mention of the fact I've gone
   organic.

Week 30
The other day I bought myself my new designer's app;
From Harrods; I was served there by a darling little
   chap,

Who installed it on my iPad (I allow myself these
   perks);
I know it will be useful . . . once I've found out how it
   works.

But then I've always understood designers' little
   tricks;
When you wear Max Mara and Chanel you've bought
   from Harvey Nicks,

You develop quite an eye for form and colour, taste and
   style;
My friends say often that my garden plans stand out a
   mile

From the ones we see at Chelsea when we tour the
   Flower Show;
I meet them at the Gala – it's the only time to go,

On Monday evening with the men who stand and talk
   in huddles;
We ladies drink champagne and look at gardens,
   dodging puddles.

Week 35

Letitia said my courtyard plan for hers in Little Venice
Is the best ten thousand pounds she's spent since
     learning to play tennis.

I worried about charging; it's a risk I have to take.
Guy says his reputation and the school's is what's at
     stake.

He seemed quite pleased and smiley when Serena (so
     good looking)
Was commissioned by a Saudi Prince in Esher – quite
     some booking.

In fact, Guy said he'd tag along to see it turned out fine.
He does that quite a lot I've noticed – never, though,
     with mine.

Week 40

I'm struggling with the Latin names, and Lottie's little
     pond
Has sprung a leak, she's furious and not remotely fond

Of the planting on the terrace, which she says has holes
     and gaps;

I blame the garden centre. They sent down two surly
chaps,

Who altered all my planting schemes and put in
substitutes.
Their ghastly things in three-inch pots had hardly any
roots.

Week 45

Reluctantly, I've left the course (Guy did not make a
fuss).
I've noticed, with Serena, he refers to them as 'us'.

Perhaps, upon reflection, I'd have been far better off
Interior designing – then I'd not have got this cough

From spending hours bent double planting stuff in
Lottie's border;
She told a friend, quite brutally, 'I simply can't afford
her.'

Week 50

The iPad I have given to my cleaner's younger son;
He uses it for war games and I hope he has more fun

Than I did during that whole ghastly, sordid episode;
I'm done with my short-lived career, and Guy, the little
   toad.

He's shacked up with Serena now. We'll see how that
   one ends . . .
And Lottie's cut me dead in Prada – so much for one's
   friends . . .

Week 52
I'm feeling rather better since I packed the whole lot
   in;
I concentrate on Pilates, Feng Shui, Mindfulness . . .
   and gin.

Next week I fly out to Gstadt for a healthy mini-break.
Rupert can't come with me, but I doubt I'll be awake

After shopping in the boutiques, having facials and hot
   stones;
I think I've earned it, anyway; I can feel it in my bones.

I never was cut out to be a girl with a career.
Would I recommend it to you? No bloody fear!

Solace

When the worries of the world engulf me;
When doubt gnaws into my soul;
When the world seems grey and bleached of colour;
When anxiety tightens its fist around my heart;
When my stomach is knotted and I know not why;
When my head is just too full of disparate thoughts;
When man's carelessness leads me to despair;
When my sense of proportion is skewed;
When bitterness begins to eat away at me;
When a sense of perspective is hard to cling to through
  the mist;
When grief undermines my equilibrium;
When anger rises in my breast;
And when I hurt;
I go out into my garden, where my spirits rise
And the world is bathed again in sunshine or washed
  by cleansing rain.

Things that Lift my Spirits

The blackbird's early evening song on the chimneypot
Walking on dew-laden grass with bare feet
Spring growth on topiary
The scent of lilac
The sound of gently bubbling water
The first brimstone butterfly of spring
New potatoes
Mowing
New-laid eggs for breakfast
The first April asparagus
Sun through newly unfurled beech leaves
Hearing the thrush breaking open a snail shell
The smell of rain on parched soil
Michaelmas daisies in autumn
Cowslips in the spring meadow
Cherry blossom
The first cuckoo calling over the valley
Feeding the wild fish in the pond
Sitting outside with that first cup of tea early on a
    summer morning

The scent of old-fashioned roses

Newly arrived swallows wheeling over the barn

Tulips

The sound of my grandchildren laughing in the garden

For all these I smile and am grateful to be a
   gardener . . .

IF YOU GO out visiting stately homes and gardens, you'll enjoy the infinite riches of British garden history – much of it inspired by the kings and queens of England, who were among the earliest patrons of plant collectors sent to the far corners of the globe to bring back botanical riches.

Such voyages took place in the sixteenth century, when Henry VIII and Elizabeth I occupied the throne. I've always been astonished at how much Elizabeth travelled around the land – we are told with a court of around 2,000 people. No wonder she bankrupted many a country squire.

Or did she really travel as much as the stately guide-books would have us believe?

Good Queen Bess

'Elizabeth the First slept here in 1582.'

I question the veracity. Is this always true?

Elizabeth the First, we're told, oft slept away from
   home;

I've done a calculation, allowing her to roam;

But by my careful reckoning – from Longleat to The
   Vyne –

Bess departed from this life aged two hundred and
   nine.

SOMETIMES IT IS the simplest and the commonest things in life that give us the greatest pleasure. So it is with the blackbird. His song from the chimney tops was one of my *Desert Island Discs* when I was asked to choose my eight records umpteen years ago.

It would still be among those eight today. It never palls.

The Blackbird

He lands, he cocks his tail, he clears his throat and
    sings;
The blackbird is oblivious to the pleasure that he
    brings.
There upon the chimney pot the avian choirboy trills;
Rippling notes of plangency that banish all my ills.

Why does he sing so freely? A territorial call?
Or is he bursting just to say, 'I'm happy with it all'?
The triteness of this sentiment can't tarnish his delight;
He does not care a fig as day turns slowly into night.

I listen, rapt; his clarion call re-echoes all around;
As crotchet, quaver, minim from the shingled spire
    rebound.
No spire his perch, no lofty tower, but just my chimney
    stack.
He knows, perhaps, his rightful place – he is no
    lumberjack.

No artist in the opera house, no soaring coloratura,
Can claim her vocalising is, compared with blackbird,
  purer.
No orchestra, no maestro – as our diva has – to tell her
The how and what and when to sing; he's happy *a
  capella.*

Not for him analysis by worthy musicologist;
Neither is his gift explained by any ornithologist.
He sings at suppertime and then flies off to roost and
  slumber;
His works are fully improvised and need no Köchel
  number.

The daylight fades, the evening's blush of copper stains
  the sky;
There's just one last cadenza, a litany for day gone by.
And then, the anthem over, he wings his way back
  home;
I smile and murmur 'Thank you' and prepare for night
  to come.

I FIRMLY BELIEVE that the ability to grow things is present in all of us – it is a natural and native aptitude. That said, it is buried very deeply in some people and rarely makes it to the surface. I blame technology, which has turned most human beings into spectators rather than participants where an involvement with nature and the land is concerned.

This state of affairs gives rise, in my case, to conversations that often run on these lines:

Brown Fingers

'I can't grow anything,' she said.

'I kill everything.

'I only have to look at it and it dies.'

'But did you really look at it?' I ask.

'I mean, long enough to notice if it looked happy or unhappy?'

'What do you mean?'

'Plants look happy or unhappy.'

'That's silly!' she said.

'Perhaps that's why you can't grow anything.'

She looked at me as though I were deranged.

'They want to grow,' I said.

'They only need three things: water, light and a suitable temperature.'

'It's not rocket science, is it?' her voice is tinged with sarcasm.

'No. It's gardening.'

'Funny how I can't do it, isn't it?'

'Hilarious.'

THEN THERE ARE those who are terrified of a garden; who regard it as a burden or, worse, as something to be totally ignored or used as storage space for broken white goods.

Oh, it makes me weep at the missed opportunity . . .

What is a Garden?

Can somebody please tell me what a garden's meant to
be?
Some see it as a dreary chore; that someone isn't me.

Some like it clean and sterile, paved with coloured
concrete blocks;
They're happy if it's tidy – rather like a drawer of socks.

Others never venture out till Easter sun is shining;
The winter is for Caribbean temperatures reclining

On a padded, pampered sunbed being offered cool
mojitos;
A pleasant change from garden ponds just swarming
with mosquitoes

On those summer days they do set out to potter in the
garden,
Then their hands develop calluses and arteries start to
harden

Thanks to letting it get 'out of hand' or 'wilding' as they
    call it;
Reluctant to pay hired help to get stuck in and haul it

Back to something cultivated, pleasant and relaxing;
But digging, forking, hoeing weeds they find just far
    too taxing.

Instead they'll opt for gravel and a patio neatly
    decked;
They wonder why no wildlife visits – what do they
    expect?

The birds and bees and butterflies like flowers that
    have nectar;
It's no use planting double blooms, unless you just
    expect a

Technicolor riot of magenta, red and blue;
All frightfully jolly, visually, but wildlife has no clue

Just what to do with petals that are there instead of
    pollen;
They need to feed on nectar both in London and
    Llangollen.

So get stuck in and look upon your little piece of earth
As a chance to make a difference – it's time for your
    rebirth

As a fully-fledged participant in nature's celebration,
And if every baffled being right across our glorious
    nation

Got to grips with their own patch of soil from
    Woolacombe to Wick;
The NHS would soon discover fewer folk were sick,

Thanks to exercise and good clean air. You got the
    message yet?
Please . . . leave your chair, and walk out there, and
    stop being so wet.

MANY OF US remember a time when butterflies were in plentiful supply and when our gardens were awash with them in summer. The over-use of chemicals, the disappearance of their habitats and the food plants of the caterpillars (as distinct from the nectar-bearing flowers beloved of the butterflies themselves) have led to a rapid decline, not only in the number of butterflies we see each year, but also in the species that we can call native.

It is generally accepted that today we have only fifty-eight species of British native butterflies; these are they:

British Butterflies

Large and Small Whites we all know and just say:
  'Cabbage White';
The Orange Tip is brighter and a cheery, welcome sight;
It lays its eggs on cuckoo flower – known as ladies
  smock;
The Green-veined White is rarer and the Brimstone
  quite a shock
When with overwintered Tortoiseshells, Red Admirals,
  Painted Ladies
It disports itself in gardens with the grace of a
  Mercedes.
The Skippers are a speckled breed – eight of them in
  all:
The Chequered, Essex, Grizzled, Lulworth, Dingy, oh,
  and Small.
The Silver Spotted's very rare – found on the Dorset
  coast;
The Large is more ubiquitous – the one you'll see the
  most.
Elusive is the word that's used in talk of Swallowtails,

They're mainly found in Norfolk, with variants in South
Wales.

No one mentions Wood Whites, but then they are
localised,

And Clouded Yellows *come* in clouds and find us quite
surprised,

Since they visit us from Europe, when they feel like
popping over;

They flit through hedge and meadowland to lay their
eggs on clover.

The hairstreaks – there are four of them – you'll find
throughout the land:

White Letter, Green, Brown, Purple – they're a jolly,
varied band.

But like so many families who live off the beaten track,

They have a wayward relative, you've guessed it, he's
the Black

Sheep of the family living on the Chiltern Hills;

Feeds on blackthorn (did you guess?) and never pays
his bills.

Small Copper caterpillars feed on sorrel – sometimes
broad-leafed dock,

They just don't like the North of Scotland (very sorry,
Jock!).

The Blues are so romantic – tiny, flitting fast and loose;

Try to get a closer look before they just vamoose.

The Chalkhill, Silver-studded, Small, and there's the
    Holly, too,

Which lays its summer eggs on ivy (I love that, don't
    you?).

The Common Blue is everywhere, just as its name
    suggests;

Adonis Blues are in the south 'expanding north and
    west'.

The Large Blue is the rarest and at one time quite
    extinct,

But now it makes a comeback since we've found that it
    is linked

To the lifestyle of a little ant that burrows under thyme

On grassland that's acidic or is growing over lime

Stone on the coasts where ants enjoy a life that's by the
    sea.

Which brings me to Fritillaries – the Duke of Burgundy

Is one I've not set eyes on yet – my hopes have not
    been quashed,

I love the Small Pearl-bordered and the graceful Silver-
    washed.

There's the ordinary Pearl-bordered, the High Brown
    and the Dark Green;

Each of them is chequered in the daintiest pattern seen.

The Marsh and Heath Fritillaries are such a welcome
    sight,
The Glanville is the rarest – on the Channel Isles and
    Wight.
You might think the 'Brown Argus' would contain the
    daily news,
The Northern and the Scotch Argus have similar russet
    hues.
Such names confuse the novice, to whom the Peacock is
    a bird,
The Comma? A punctuation mark; now isn't that absurd?
The Wall is never made of bricks, nor is the Speckled
    Wood,
The Grayling is no politician – glad that's understood.
The Small Heath and the Large Heath don't refer to
    Tory Ted
In varying size of trousers, nor the party that he led.
The Marbled White's not made of stone, nor has the
    Ringlet tresses;
You'll find her in most counties at most countryside
    addresses.
Small Mountain Ringlets are more picky, found up in
    the Lakes;
And in Scotland – they need something, too, for
    heaven's sakes!

The Gatekeeper you'll often see – and by the garden
   fence,
The Meadow Brown is found in meadows – making
   perfect sense.
Which leaves just two – and what a pair – you'll find
   them on your rambles
In woodland where White Admirals will feed on
   flowers of brambles.
And up above, the stateliest will glide among the
   oak,
Drinking honeydew from aphids – what a dreadful
   soak.
Behold the Purple Emperor, whose praises must be
   sung,
Despite the fact that on the ground it likes to feed on
   dung.
If in your life you manage to see all our fifty-eight,
Rejoice and pop a cork to say 'three cheers' and
   celebrate.
For these are our most fragile creatures, hoping to
   survive
Midst motorways and HS2 and all of us who drive
Our diesel cars and motorbikes and fly away at will
With little thought to what our needs can injure or can
   kill.

I hope my grandchildren will know their beauty and
  their worth
And look on nettles, watching as a Tortoiseshell gives
  birth
To eighty eggs laid on a leaf in just about an hour;
Resulting in bright butterflies that flit from flower to
  flower.

Our world would be a duller place without these 'flying
  flowers'.
Their future now depends on us; the duty it is ours.

MY WIFE AND I have owned both dogs and cats over the years and love them both in equal measure. Dogs have masters, cats have slaves, but no matter, they have both proved wonderful company. That said, cats are harder for many folk to love and are frequently accused of having a detrimental effect on our native bird life.

What's more, they always seem to prefer the garden next door when it comes to performing their ablutions – something that drives even cat lovers to distraction. They have the stealth of Hiawatha and, in this case, the metre, too.

The Prowler

Softly treading through the hedgerow comes the errant
    carnivore;
Silent, watchful, sly and focused; could it be the Tom
    next door?

Turning back on home and owner, Tibbles ventures o'er
    the fence;
Creeps through bushes, careful, cautious, laundered
    whiskers ever tense.

Stops a moment, staring forward, fixing with hypnotic
    gaze
Intended quarry swiftly spotted; concentration naught
    can faze.

Piercing eyes, now downward facing, watch as paw
    begins to scratch
At fresh-tilled earth, a hollow making; mood intense as
    Cumberbatch.

Dented soil is then inspected; depth and width are soon
  approved;
Tibbles squats, with concentration, feline bowels now
  are moved.

Impassive gaze as job progresses, little sign of joy or
  pain;
Paw once more moves soil to cover newly buggered-up
  terrain.

Sometime later comes the gardener, hoping for a sign
  of growth
On the seedbed raked and watered . . . sees the carnage,
  mutters oath.

Tibbles now, on next door's terrace, sleeps upon the
  sun-warmed floor;
Hunger sated, bowels voided, dreaming of the girl next
  door.

Siamese with perfect figure, slim of waist and long of
  limb,
Eyes of blue and ears seal-pointed, clearly destined just
  for him.

Would that we his life could mirror, naught but sex and
  food and bowel
Occupying every moment, with no thought of spade or
  trowel.

You can pray in church and chapel, mosque and abbey,
  synagogue;
Nothing stops marauding moggies – unless, of course,
  you get a dog.

FAMILIES COME TOGETHER at Christmas, and gathering evergreens on Sunday walks is one way of celebrating yuletide. The holly remains the stalwart, even if mistletoe yields rather more exciting results.

The Christmas Wreath

Through frozen snow our footsteps crunch,
Setting out to cut a bunch
Of holly for the Christmas lunch.

Scarlet fruits, their brilliant livery
Cheering children cold and shivery
Waiting Santa's Yule delivery.

Decorating bird and barrel,
Showing off their gay apparel
Called to mind in verse and carol.

Fending off our wintry woe
With ivy and with mistletoe
Held aloft with Christmas bow.

No pudding stuffed with plum and fig,
No Christmas board too small or big
To benefit from holly sprig.

To do without it would be folly,
No evergreen is half as jolly
As the shining Christmas holly.

AT THE VERY heart of gardening, of growing trees and shrubs and all kinds of plants, is a knowledge that you are playing your part in the greater scheme of things. Leaving behind something beautiful and useful . . .

Seeing into the Future . . .

Have you ever planted a tree?
Yourself I mean.
When it wasn't a tree, just a sapling.
Or even smaller – a seedling perhaps?
You haven't?
Oh.
I just wondered.
It's just that when you have – pushing your spade into
    stiff earth –
And you watch it grow
For years
Until you can wrap your arms around its muscular
    trunk and pull it towards you
And it leans into you
Gently
Before it pulls away.
And deep inside you feel something strange.
Only then do you understand what the future is.
It is there.
In your embrace.

And it feels . . .

So good

So wonderful

So . . .

Worthwhile.

It took you moments.

It will outlive you

By centuries.

The Man on Earth

He leaves no mark, the man on earth,
To cause rejoicing at his birth,
Unless that mark be growing still
When he is laid 'neath yonder hill.

If at his death they cannot see
The branches of a sky-bound tree,
Whose roots he laid in leafy soil
When but a sapling, then his toil

Will count for naught in hill and dale
And vivid memory fade to pale.
But were that life to nature giv'n
Then man on earth createth heav'n
And heaven liveth evermore
Upon that tide-washed leafy shore.

FROM TIME TO time I am emboldened to take to the stage in an evening entertainment entitled, *Trowel and Error: Tales from a Life on Earth*. I cannot claim to have invented the title – that dubious honour goes to the late Sir David Frost, who once introduced me on a television quiz programme as 'a man who has made his way in life by trowel and error'. It has followed me around ever since.

In order to break the ice at the start of the evening, this tongue-in-cheek biography seems to do the trick. I have had to add a new verse each decade. There will come a time when I simply have to bow out . . .

My Story

I started at this gardening lark
When I was young and green,
Upon my granddad's cabbage patch
'Neath rows of runner bean.

And then, when I was fifteen years,
I learned it as my trade;
I mowed the grass, worked under glass
And dug and hoed and sprayed.

When I was one and twenty
I travelled down to Kew
Where, 'mongst the palms, in maiden's arms,
My passion for them grew.

When I was one and thirty
I wrote in book and mag,
And garden folk from Cheam to Stoke
Sent problems by the bag.

When I was one and forty
I gardened on the telly;
And then the post, from hill to coast,
Grew heavier and more smelly.

When I was one and fifty
(When most men buy their Harleys),
I wrote novels – long – and got my gong
And dodged those boobs of Charlie's.

When I was one and sixty
The A.T. Show had started,
And by some fluke, Queen, Prince and Duke
Into my orbit darted.

But when I'm one and seventy
I'll toddle out the door;
'Cos now that I'm a sex god
It don't matter anymore.

An invitation from the publisher

Join us at www.hodder.co.uk, or follow us
on Twitter @hodderbooks to be a part of
our community of people who love the very
best in books and reading.

Whether you want to discover more about a book
or an author, watch trailers and interviews, have the
chance to win early limited editions, or simply browse
our expert readers' selection of the very best books,
we think you'll find what you're looking for.

And if you don't, that's the place to tell us what's missing.

We love what we do, and we'd love you to be a part of it.

www.hodder.co.uk

  @hodderbooks

HodderBooks

HodderBooks